Original title:
The Life in a Terrarium

Copyright © 2025 Creative Arts Management OÜ
All rights reserved.

Author: Henry Beaumont
ISBN HARDBACK: 978-1-80581-738-3
ISBN PAPERBACK: 978-1-80581-265-4
ISBN EBOOK: 978-1-80581-738-3

The Fortress of Flora

In a glassy domain, the plants have a dance,
A fern does a jig, while the moss takes a chance.
The lizards all nod, with their scales glistening bright,
As the tiny green sprouts stage a weird little fight.

Bubbles rise up like they mean to complain,
While worms in a row form a quirky train.
The soil's a soft mattress for beetles to snooze,
In this quirky hotel, who needs to peruse?

With sunlight as laughter, and shadows as fun,
The sunflowers argue who's taller, or won.
Cacti hold meetings, they point out their pricks,
As vines start to tumble with some acrobatic tricks.

A kingdom of oddities, each day a new jest,
In a fortress of flora, it's hard not to jest.
The tiny inhabitants thrive on the cheer,
As their antics unfold, right here, crystal clear.

Tranquility in Transparent Chamber

Within this bright bubble, tranquility reigns,
The bugs play cards, ignoring their pains.
A snail writes a letter, addressed to a leaf,
While ants hold a lecture on life and belief.

The water's a mirror, where fish practice smirks,
And frogs share their gossip with well-timed quirks.
Each pebble a throne, each droplet a pearl,
In this whimsical realm where the oddities swirl.

The light-hearted breeze brings whispers of charm,
While the snails make a pact to keep things alarmed.
Cotton candy clouds float with no place to bind,
And the grass blades could giggle if only they'd find.

In a world of glass walls, hilarity grows,
Where the tiniest critters put on a grand show.
A dance floor of soil, a parade of delight,
In this whimsical chamber, all day turns to night.

Life Beneath a Clear Canopy

Beneath this glass, a little crew,
The ants throw parties, just a few.
A snail in shoes moves slow as glue,
While crickets sing a merry tune.

Tiny ferns wave like they're on stage,
While moss plays chess, directs the page.
A spider spins tales of ancient rage,
And a beetle dreams of being a mage.

Sweet Surrender to Stillness

In quiet realms of flora and cheer,
A worm does yoga, free of fear.
With tiny weights made of a leaf,
He bench-presses his ancient grief.

A spider contemplates her strands,
While lichen reads in whispered lands.
The sun's soft beams like guiding hands,
Where every speck of dust expands.

Folk Tales from a Fragmented Forest

Little creatures plot their ways,
In mini scrolls, they write their plays.
A squirrel claims he found the prize,
While fireflies dance, with flashing eyes.

Mushrooms gossip, 'Did you hear?'
About the frog who cooked with beer?
And ladybugs spread love like cheer,
Across the leaves, they persevere.

Murmurs of Nature's Nexus

Beneath the glass, a world so wry,
Where peek-a-boo beetles love to fly.
A chatty worm wants to tell the sky,
About the stars he glimpsed nearby.

Fungi laugh at their silly peers,
While raindrops play on leafy gears.
In this odd space, no room for fears,
Just punchlines tossed to bring the cheers.

Pause in the Green Sphere

Inside a glass, the plants just laugh,
They wiggle and dance, a leafy gaffe.
Tiny critters crawl, in silent delight,
'Who needs the wild when we party all night?'

A sleepy snail glides, his pace quite slow,
He dreams of adventures, but can't seem to go.
A beetle complains, 'I'm stuck in this dome,'
'Where's my chance to roam? Oh, where's my home?'

Eden in a Vessel

In a jar of green, the beetles convene,
They plot their escape, like a daring routine.
To leap from this realm, for freedom they plead,
'Oh, to frolic outside, that's the life we need!'

With mud on their feet, they gather for tea,
'Where's the point of pride in a life so free?'
One leaf whispers softly, 'Just chill where you are,'
'You'll miss all the fun of a UV bar!'

The Quiet Pulse of Photosynthesis

A shy fern blushes, under the sun,
While cacti take bets on who'll be the fun.
'Photosynthesis? What a silly deal!'
I just need a nap, that's my ideal.

As vines interlace in a muddle of green,
They giggle and curl in a ridiculous scene.
'What's that you say? It's a light party here?'
Then let's raise a cup of this liquid cheer!'

Breathing Through Transparency

In a clear house of glass, the plants have a spree,
They're hosting a ball—just my kind of glee!
A lizard waltzes with rhythm in scale,
While moss sings along, no chance to fail.

Each bubble of air is a chortle of love,
'Breathe deep, little one, it fits like a glove.'
They toast with the dew, fresh and quite zany,
'This life we've got, it's just so insane-y!'

Miniature Worlds

In a glass box, tiny bugs do tango,
Lawn chairs for ants, they dance a fandango.
Mossy carpets sprawl like giant mats,
As beetles sip tea with cool, little hats.

Rice grains scatter like pearls on the floor,
Crickets bring snacks, they all want more.
The snails in their shells discuss the best route,
While spiders spin webs—it's their time to shout!

Boundless Dreams

Cacti don hats made of sponge and fluff,
While lizards wear shades, thinking they're tough.
The rocks play cards, they're the coolest of mates,
And grasshoppers gamble, deciding their fates.

A moth tells a joke, the glowworms all giggle,
As gnomes ride the geraniums, yanking a wiggle.
The motherly fern gives advice with a frown,
Saying, 'Don't eat the dirt, it will weigh you down!'

Tales from a Living Capsule

Inhabitants here play hide and seek,
While ladybugs cheer with joy, so cheeky and sleek.
The sun shines down on their vibrant display,
As old king snail decides to delay.

The marbles around are planets so bright,
As critters soar high, in their flights of delight.
The pebbles exchange gossip about the dawn,
While the twinkling dew keeps growing long.

Verdant Realms Behind Transparent Walls

Beyond clear panes, where dreams come alive,
Tadpoles in tuxedos argue and thrive.
The butterfly bakes cakes with glittery spice,
While rabbits critique them, giving solid advice.

Hydrangeas gossip about a nearby flower,
As time ticks away—who knows the hour?
Frogs hold tight debates in the moon's soft glow,
Claiming the best seats—it's quite the show!

Beneath the Canopy of Crystal

Beneath this dome, pets do prance,
Roaming around, each bug has a chance.
The goldfish swims through a grassy sea,
While turtles keep time, dancing with glee.

Air plants shuffle just to stay in the cool,
Making new friends in this shining jewel.
With a wink and a nod, the earthworms unite,
Trading their tales in the bright morning light!

Enigma of the Ever-Greenhouse

In a jar with lid so tight,
Plants plot their daily height.
Moss whispers secrets in green code,
While ferns throw leaves down the road.

Beetles dance like they're on stage,
Cacti grumble, 'What a cage!'
Lettuce dreams of open skies,
A tomato winks with hidden lies.

The sunbeams tickle, plants start to sway,
While tiny snails dine on leaves of hay.
Bubbles from soil make a funny sound,
As critters plot their escape profound.

Together they plot, in this glassy realm,
A humorous coup, who'll take the helm?
With laughter and sunlight, their hopes are bold,
In the greenhouse of giggles, stories unfold.

Reflections of Growth in Encased Reality

Tiny wonders trapped in glass,
Boldly growing, not a moment to pass.
Fungi giggle, dress in fine lace,
While roots entwine, embrace their space.

Silly sprouts with dreams to bloom,
Plotting routes beneath the gloom.
The humidity hums a merry song,
While worms boast, 'We'll play all day long!'

In the stillness, algae conspires,
To bring forth laughter, playing with fires.
A tangle of growth, a hilarious mess,
As marbles roll and plants confess.

Peeking out from every leaf,
Are jokes that bring comic relief.
In this small world of leafy cheer,
Life's a riot, with giggles near!

Whispers of Glass Gardens

A curious frog dons a crown,
Hopping about, showing off its gown.
In the still waters, fishes joke,
While quirky stones begin to poke.

Sunlight spills, a golden flood,
Each leaf covered in a smiling bud.
The air is thick with tales and chuckles,
As critters dance and share their huddles.

Moss sketches portraits, all in jest,
While beetles gather, feeling blessed.
A pennywort sings a lullaby,
To tickle the hearts of passersby.

Bubbles pop with giggles near,
In the glassy realm, there's cheer.
Life's a party, come take a glance,
Among whispering leaves, we'll all dance!

Secrets Beneath the Soil

Down below, the roots conspire,
Whispering secrets of love and fire.
Earthworms tell tales of a hefty meal,
While fungi giggle at every squeal.

The beetles meet for a potluck feast,\nPreparing snacks that never cease.
With carrots dreaming of a grand parade,
A rooty rave in the soil they've laid.

Each little hire in the dirt so deep,
Offers chuckles that make you leap.
In shadows where the funny things dwell,
Life's a riddle that's hard to tell.

Come join the laughter, hear the cheer,
Where mischief blooms and plants persevere.
In the darkness, jokes are in play,
As nature laughs at the light of day!

A Versicle of Verdure

In glassy halls where ferns do dance,
The tiny bugs take every chance.
A beetle winks, a snail gives chase,
What a curious, little race!

The mossy mats, they joke and tease,
While spider webs snag gentle breeze.
A glimpse of life in tiny space,
Oh, nature's funny little place!

With droopy leaves that seem to pout,
They whisper secrets, shout, and sprout.
A critter lands—a party guest,
Who knew plants could be so blessed?

A waterfall of faux, not real,
The pebbles laugh, the lids conceal.
In this green world, hilarity grows,
With every turn, another show!

Tales from a Jewel of Life

In a crystal box, so snug and bright,
The tiny shapes twist left and right.
A ladybug wears spiffy boots,
While ants compete in fancy suits.

The soil grumbles, says, "Not fair,
Why don't you wear a hipster hair?"
The carrots giggle, point and stare,
At veggies dressed in debonair!

Those fronds are gossiping, oh so loud,
Making fun of a passing cloud.
Lettuce lounges, cool and chill,
In this jewel, a world to thrill!

With every root, a joke unfolds,
In leafy tales, absurd and bold.
Each little scene, a laugh parade,
In nature's gem, the fun won't fade!

The Subtle Art of Seclusion

Behind the glass, a secret laugh,
A turtle's on a tiny path.
He stops to ponder, then gets lost,
Forgetting all at nature's cost!

The pebbles gossip, talk a lot,
About the plants, who's doing what.
"Did you see the moss's new hairstyle?"
They chuckle softly for a while.

A fairy quest, it seems, unfolds,
With sparkling dreams and treasures told.
A snail in boots joins in the fun,
Proclaiming, "Look! I'm quite the run!"

Each tiny creature plays a role,
In this glass world, everyone's whole.
With winks and grins, a secret place,
Where quiet quirks declare their grace!

Fragrant Footnotes in a Terrarium

Amidst the greens, a fragrance grows,
A lavender wave that tickles noses.
A rogue sprout struts with swagger proud,
Inviting all to join the crowd!

The cactus jests, "I'm so unique!
With prickles sharp, I'm not for the weak!"
The flowers giggle as they bloom,
In this green, fragrant, tiny room.

Each morning dew, a glistened tease,
As snails parade down leafy seas.
"Who needs a spa when you have this?
A little water is pure bliss!"

Laughter echoes through the vine,
As dragonflies sip on sweet sunshine.
Each moment here, a joyful scheme,
In this miniature, fragrant dream!

A Dance of Moss and Light

A mossy stage for tiny feet,
Where sunlight winks at roots so sweet.
The ferns twirl in playful glee,
While beetles hum a symphony.

In glassy walls, the laughter flows,
As snails practice their graceful pose.
With each tiny hop, a joyful cheer,
Who knew the jungle could be so near?

The pebbles roll, a comical dance,
While worms wiggle, given a chance.
A world where giggles softly bloom,
Under the glass, a living room.

Each leaf a partner, swaying so fine,
With nature's quirks, it's all divine.
So, join the fun in this green delight,
Where every day feels just right!

The Hidden Ballet of Botanicals

In secret stages, the plants obey,
To choreographed moves in the light of day.
Tiny critters take center stage,
With roots and leaves, they engage.

The soil giggles, a playful ground,
As butterflies twirl, dancing around.
Unseen antics, they spin and glide,
In this glassy dome, there's nowhere to hide.

A ladybug dons a tutu bright,
While crickets play tunes deep into the night.
With each little hop, they bring us cheer,
A botanical ballet is always near.

In shadows cast by fronds so lush,
A tiny world, with glee and hush.
So take a peek, don't let it pass,
Where flora pirouettes on a bed of grass!

Harmony in a Closed Ecosystem

In a world behind glass, laughter sings,
With critters mingling, oh the joy it brings!
The whispers of leaves as they gently sway,
Tell secrets of laughter in their own way.

The beetles bicker about who's the best,
While crickets conduct a nightly fest.
The mosses giggle, their colors bright,
Painting the walls in the soft moonlight.

A dance of shadows, a joyful show,
As droplets shimmer, they put on a glow.
Every inch of this marvel, a playful tease,
Where nature's spirits dance with ease.

So peer inside, don't blink or miss,
The harmony here is a silly bliss.
In each little corner, a tale is spun,
In this glassy haven, the fun's never done!

Stories of the Enclosed

Behind the glass, tales unfold,
Of tiny lives, both bright and bold.
The ants have meetings, planning their day,
While a curious snail slowly makes its way.

With tiny gestures and a lively cheer,
Every creature seems to hold dear.
The ferns gossip, the moss holds sway,
In this whimsical world, they laugh and play.

A tiny beetle crafts insect art,
While crazy crickets break into a cart.
Each leaf a page in this comic book,
Come sit and smile, take a good look!

The drama unfolds in this playful dome,
Where every little creature feels right at home.
So peek inside and bring your grin,
For the stories here are just about to begin!

Life's Cradle of Containment

A turtle wedged among the moss,
Gathers gossip like a boss.
"Did you hear about the snail?"
"Took a ride on a little rail!"

The grapevine twists with leafy jokes,
While parakeets put on their cloaks.
They dance beneath the glassy dome,
Next to the mushrooms that call it home.

The beetles strut in fancy suits,
While spiders spin their loop-de-loops.
A bumblebee brings news of cheer,
"No winter here! Just sun and beer!"

In corners where the mist might creep,
The dryads play hide and seek.
Who'd have thought a jar so small,
Could hold this circus, after all!

Fragments of Ferny Dreams

In a world of plants and tiny things,
A frog dreams loud, and the echo rings.
"To leap or not, that is the quest!"
As he sits snug, a well-fed guest.

The ferns laugh softly, swaying low,
While the garden gnome steals the show.
"Don't step on me! I'm fragile too!"
Says a daisy with a point of view.

A wise old snail on a pebble high,
Declares it's time for a cupcake pie.
"Let's plant the seeds of fun today!"
Betty the bug just winks, "Hooray!"

Tiny glows from fireflies buzz,
As they dance around, oh what a fuss!
In this glass, the joy's supreme,
Life's a spectacle, or so it seems!

Whispers Among the Stones

Behind a rock, the lizards speak,
Their chatter makes the frogs all weak.
"Did you hear the crickets' tale?"
"They're throwing quite the nighttime gala!"

A snail scribbles a new best-seller,
"How to win friends, even in a cellar!"
His fans roll out, with ample cheer,
Saying, "We love you, pioneer!"

Nearby, the ants are crafting schemes,
While twigs and leaves form their dreams.
"Join our march! It's a solid plan!"
Says the ant with a tiny can.

In shadows deep where secrets loom,
The mushrooms giggle beneath the gloom.
They whisper tales that twist and bend,
In the kingdom where the fun won't end!

Clockwork of the Closed System

Tick-tock goes the tiny clock,
Where the goldfish spins like a rock.
"Is it noon or is it dusk?"
The hamster wheels feel somewhat brusque.

Rabbits plot a wily race,
To see who'll win the silliest chase.
"Catch me if you can!" they cheer,
While the parakeet calls, "Disengage fear!"

Clock hands wobble in delight,
As insects plan their swarm tonight.
"A fiesta on the wooden floor,"
Says the pill bug, while they adore.

What a world where puns do thrive,
And every creature feels alive.
In this jar, with laughter abloom,
Who needs the wild? We've got our room!

Journeying Through a Pocket Paradise

In a jar where greens can thrive,
Tiny beings dance and jive.
Mossy carpets, a leafy spread,
Who knew plants could have such cred?

A ladybug plays hide and seek,
While a slug comes out for a peek.
Each leaf whispers a tiny tale,
In this home where critters nail.

The Stillness of Cultivated Chaos

A jungle forged in glass so bright,
Fluffy ferns greet morning light.
Cacti wear their spiky crowns,
While snails glide without a sound.

A spider spins a web so neat,
Attention seeking from her seat.
Each twist a dance in nature's show,
In a place where wild things grow.

Echoes of Earth in a Sealed Space

Amongst the soil and tangled roots,
An ant debates his tiny pursuits.
'Is this my world?' he seems to muse,
As a beetle shares the news he'd lose.

Crystal droplets on glass walls cling,
Nature's whispers make us sing.
One cheeky worm takes center stage,
As the crowd cheers, it's all the rage!

Fragments of Nature in a Controlled Climate

Inside this glassy little dome,
A gnome says, 'Welcome to my home!'
With wilted leaves as dinner guests,
It seems this place is all the bests.

Behold the dance of shadows low,
As tiny plants put on a show.
In such a small, enchanted plot,
Life's strange antics hit the spot.

Gazing into Green Realms

In a glassy world, plants twist and play,
Tiny trees strut in their leafy ballet.
Frogs hop and croak, a comical choir,
As snails take their time, never in a hurry.

Mossy carpets cushion each small, fat root,
Songs of the soil in a green suit.
Bugs in tuxedos dance on the glass,
While worms throw a party—oh, what a gas!

Sunlight beams down like a disco light,
Dancing shadows bring life to the night.
The tiny ones giggle, oh what a sight,
In this quirky world, everything feels right.

A drop of water brings confetti rain,
While little leaves cheer, without any pain.
In this lively realm, laughter is key,
Who knew a jar could be so funny?

Harbors of Hope and Harmony

In a jar that's round, a universe glows,
Tiny plants tremble, in a breeze that blows.
Fluffy clouds of moss, all soft and nice,
While creatures debate: who's next for dice?

A toad in a corner, with a hat just so,
Claims he's the king of this verdant show.
Frogs play charades, they leap and they dive,
With each little croak, we all feel alive.

The sunlight spills smiles through each green maze,
As ants march in line, holding their gaze.
With tiny umbrellas, they're ready for rain,
In this harbor of hope, there's never a drain.

A cheerful whisper, the breeze tells a tale,
Of adventures untold on a miniature scale.
In harmony's dance, all creatures unite,
Each day is a play, a wonderful sight!

Sprouts of Serenity

Little sprouts giggle with all of their might,
As raindrops tap dance, oh what a sight!
Tiny roots whisper secrets so sweet,
In this calm abode, where nature meets.

A gnome with a grin digs for treasure by chance,
While critters unite in a lively dance.
Ladybugs twirl with a flick of their wings,
In this peaceful offering, joy truly sings.

Silly mushrooms wear hats, all mismatched,
As lizards play chess on a leaf so detached.
The sun bows low, painting shadows that sway,
In this realm where laughter decides the play.

With each gentle breeze, mischief's afoot,
Tiny critters giggle, oh aren't they cute?
In this serene nest, hilarity blooms,
Where every little laugh just brightens the rooms!

Visions from Vital Vessels

Within glassy confines, antics unfold,
A scene so alive, it never gets old.
The cactus sings ballads, prickly but bold,
While busy beetles plot stories retold.

Stretching and yawning, the ferns all complain,
Why is it always the same silly game?
With whispers of joy in the leaves up high,
These vital vessels, oh my, oh my!

The sunlight winks, like a jester in glee,
Bringing bright laughter to all, even me!
A hamster in a wheel waves 'hello' with style,
While snails take their time, flaunting their smile.

Jars filled with wonders, no reason to sigh,
As creatures unite, under the bright sky.
Together they thrive in this comical play,
In vessels of life, each day is a sway!

Nature's Own Terrific Theater

In a glass box, the show begins,
Tiny critters wearing fins.
A snail in costume, what a sight,
Dancing awkwardly in the light.

A spider struts, a diva's flair,
With legs like ribbons in the air.
The plants sway, they love the beat,
Rooted there, they tap their feet.

A frog joins in, a croaking tone,
His serenade is all his own.
The audience? Just a curious cat,
Wondering, "What's with all this chat?"

As the curtain falls, the lights go dim,
The critters take a bow, on a whim.
Tomorrow's show is sure to please,
With more antics from the trees!

Hush of the Hidden Habitat

In a quiet world beneath the lid,
A worm is plotting, oh how he hid!
With his pals, the ants, in low-key chats,
Planning a feast with some fallen hats.

Mossy boulders, they hold a summit,
"Who ate the lettuce? Come on, just admit!"
The ladybugs laugh, with spots all bright,
"Not us, dear friends, we're on a diet tonight!"

A cricket strums a lullaby tune,
While the cactus sighs under the moon.
The leftovers are too good to waste,
As the critters gather for a midnight feast.

Under the cover of leaves and dirt,
A hidden laugh escapes the earth.
In this small world, chaos is sweet,
Where every day, they dance and eat!

Glass Enclaves of Verdancy

Beyond the glass, the world is bright,
Within, the drama's pure delight.
A turtle sprawls in a sunny patch,
While a lizard looks for a perfect match.

The ferns gossip about the gloom,
"Did you see that bug? He's got no zoom!"
With laughter bubbling from the brook,
It's all in good fun, take a look!

The beetles race, a silly spree,
"Not so fast! You're cheating me!"
While moss makes soft beds for the weary,
Collecting tales that are quite cheery.

As light fades, they wind down the day,
With funny whispers and games to play.
In this enclave where green reigns supreme,
It's a wacky world, or so it seems!

Oasis of the Ordinary

In a cozy nook, the critters lounge,
Beneath the leaves, they play and scrounge.
A goldfish dreams of skies so wide,
While a hamster rides a beetle's side.

"Let's have a race!" the locust shouts,
Over twigs and pebbles, roundabout routes.
The results, of course, are a complete mess,
But laughter erupts, who cares? No stress!

The plants giggle, they wobble in fun,
As the sun dips low, and the day is done.
With tiny cheers, they bid goodnight,
In this ordinary place, there's pure delight!

Tomorrow brings a brand new plan,
More adventures, as only they can.
In this oasis, life unfolds bright,
Filled with giggles and pure delight!

Serenity within Silica

Little plants all lined in rows,
They wave to the snails, striking poses.
A dance in glass, with soil so fine,
Who knew greens could throw such a shine?

Bubbles rise like laughter, oh dear!
The air's so still, it's almost sheer.
Tiny birds chirp but stay on the shelf,
Not a soul here can talk to itself!

A pop of color, a speck of dirt,
All these critters just think they're curt.
Is that a frog or a mask of clay?
In this lively world, we skip and sway!

So grab a seat, enjoy the show,
Where everyone's friendly, no seeds of woe.
In our glass stage, we giggle and grow,
Who knew that plants could steal the show?

Echoes in a Sealed World

A busy bug hops on a twig,
"Oh no," he says, "I'm feeling big!"
In a world so small, he cannot hide,
"No room for stunts, it's too confined!"

The ants march on, a silent parade,
Silly little legs with street plans laid.
Each leaf a stage for a curious spy,
Who knew such antics could make time fly?

A snail just laughs at the frantic race,
"I'll win this game at my own pace!"
The critters chuckle, what a delight,
In this sealed chamber, all's out of sight!

So here begins the quirkiest play,
Where entertainers brighten the day.
In echoes soft behind the glass wall,
Who knew it'd be such a bouncy ball?

Tiny Kingdoms of Green

In this tiny land, a ruler looms,
An odd little plant with grand blooms.
Its throne made of soil, it reigns supreme,
Oh, how it dreams while others beam!

The mushrooms giggle, their hats look grand,
They plot a party—they've got a band!
A mossy dance floor, a foggy stage,
Our little empire sets the page!

With tiny flags made of blades so bright,
They wave at the sun with all their might.
Each day a fest, with food on the ground,
Who knew such fun could yet be found?

So gather around in this small domain,
Where laughter grows like the plants in the rain.
In our cute kingdom, we all unite,
Sipping on drops of dew, pure delight!

Beneath the Dome of Dreams

In a dome so round, with a radiant glow,
We host a circus, come see the show!
A beetle on a seesaw, quite the thrill,
It teeters and totters, cannot stay still!

Look at the goldfish, oh what a sight,
They bubble with jokes, all day and night.
A cactus with quips? What a delight!
"Just prickle away!" it gives pure fright!

Here's a worm in a hat, playing coy,
"Oh dear!" it squeaks, "I'm just a toy!"
The world of whimsy, under glass so clear,
Who knew imagination could float so near?

Now raise a toast to this wacky crew,
In our tiny space, there's room for you.
It's a bubbly blast where laughter streams,
So welcome aboard, beneath our dreams!

Untold Tales from Terra's Heart

Once a snail with dreams so grand,
He plotted journeys, planned and planned.
Yet all he saw was just a leaf,
His travel tales are quite the grief.

A sprightly ant with shoes so bright,
Claimed every leftover as her right.
She danced around her veggie throne,
Proclaiming all the greens her own.

A chatty plant with leafy flair,
Spoke to a rock—oh, what a pair!
In whispered tones, they planned a scheme,
To grow a garden, live the dream.

So here inside this glassy maze,
Life's quirks unfold in funny ways.
From tiny worlds we chuckle loud,
In terra's heart, we feast and crowd.

Worlds within Walls

In a jar where critters dwell,
A worm spins tales, a strange carousel.
He twists and wriggles, proud and slick,
But oh, the plight of being quick!

A spider weaves both web and jest,
Claiming her corner as the best.
She spins her stories with such grace,
Yet fears the dust that leaves a trace.

Frogs in beads of green do thrive,
Croaking songs to feel alive.
Yet every leap is quite the show,
With slips and trips that steal the glow.

Within these walls, a mishap waits,
As every critter dreams of dates.
Together here, we laugh and play,
In worlds of flora, every day.

Hallowed Halls of Hydroponics

In sacred soil, a lettuce sighs,
As radishes tell, "Look at us rise!"
They chat about their leafy fate,
While plotting ways to break the gate.

Cucumbers lounge, embracing the light,
They gossip of roots, and such a sight!
With every vine, they twist and share,
Plans for a salad—but beware!

Parsnips parade in their earthy coat,
Claiming together they can float.
But wobbly roots can topple tales,
And soon they find they've lost their trails.

In hallowed halls where seedlings sprout,
The humor grows without a doubt.
From whispered dreams in playful space,
Life thrives here, at a jolly pace.

Breath of Life Encased

Inside this globe, a frog holds court,
With jests about a lost report.
His lily pad, a throne so grand,
Where every leap is bravely planned.

A bug with shades sits back in style,
Mocks the plants with every smile.
"Who needs the sun? I'm cool," he brags,
While dodging raindrops in the rags.

The mossy patch, all soft and stewy,
Attempts to tell a joke quite gooey.
But every punchline turns to green,
A giggly mess that must be seen.

Encased in glass, we find our groove,
Where laughter dances, plants will move.
In this small world of fun and mirth,
Each breath a joy, each giggle worth.

Chronicles of the Enclaved

Inside my bubble, plants do dance,
They prance like kids, given half a chance.
But when the cat comes, oh what a fright,
They're all in hiding, clinging on tight.

Little ferns plot with their leafy might,
Planning an escape under cover of night.
But then the sun shines, warmth beams down,
And they giggle, forgetting the frown.

Curly vines twist, a tangled delight,
Messy green hair, what a hilarious sight!
The snail, slowpoke, takes his sweet time,
In a race with a leaf, such a silly crime.

Each day unfolds like a comic strip,
With butterfly photos, on summer's trip.
When growing gets tough, they take it in stride,
'Tis just a normal day inside their glass tide.

Glimpses of Verdant Survival

These plants live large in their glassy dome,
A sporting arena, not merely a home.
The moss whispers secrets, the soil does chuckle,
As earthworms wiggle, forming a huddle.

A cactus dreams of a beach holiday,
While succulents laugh, "You've got sunburned today!"
Hydrangeas gossip, their petals held high,
"Oh darling, did you see? That bug made her cry!"

The humidity rises, the laughter gets tense,
They argue 'bout watering—who's got the sense?
With a pinch of soil, and a drop of cheer,
They're the best of jesters, a riotous sphere.

With every small tune from the light pouring in,
They twirl and they whirl, like they're all in a spin.
In their glassy world, the humor's full bloom,
A comedic garden, a botanical room.

Botanicals Bound in Glass

In a jar so shiny, the leaves regale,
Each inch a sensation, a botanical tale.
The critters creep in, staged a little play,
With spiky plants grumbling, 'Hey, not today!'

The moss jokes about its green fuzzy hair,
"More like a perm, let's all beware!"
While succulents tease, with their plump little cheeks,
"Life's too short, eat dirt for a week!"

A ladybug waves, wearing polka-dot pride,
Saying, "I'm the queen here, you all must abide!"
Petunias twist petals, making a fuss,
"Let's organize a bloom, without any rush!"

The tiny terrarium thrives with delight,
In their snug enclosure, all laughs take flight.
With sunshine above and laughter below,
Those fragile green giggles continue to grow.

Sojourn in Nature's Capsule

Captured in glass, the laughter is thick,
Tiny plants chat, they've all got their shtick.
A fragile ballet, with roots tap dancing,
Frogs play the piano, while the leaves are prancing.

A creeping vine tells tales of the past,
Of moonlit soirees that could never last.
As bugs send postcards from their little camps,
They giggle at humans—big silly tramps!

Cucumbers whisper, "Where's my lunch?"
While radishes ponder, "Just one little crunch?"
The terrarium's bustling, a green little maze,
Filled with tiny ruckus and cheeky green plays.

They peek through the glass at the big world outside,
Wishing for outings, to stretch and to slide.
But for now, my friends, let's enjoy this space,
In our glassy abode, we've found our own grace.

A Symphony of Small Growths

In a jar where all the tiny things stay,
Funky fungi dance, making their own way.
Moss on a mission, with gusto they thrive,
Chasing the sunlight, feeling so alive.

Worms wear hats, made of old lettuce peel,
And the ants tap dance, oh, what a big deal!
Each leaf has a story, each sprout has its quirks,
In this mini jungle, where everyone works.

Bubbles of laughter, air plants take a leap,
Peeking at the world, their secrets to keep.
Frogs wear tuxedos, ready for the ball,
While crickets sing loudly, proclaiming it all.

The ladybugs giggle, with spots of delight,
As they twirl and they sway, from morning to night.
It's a ruckus of green, a spectacle grand,
In a glassy domain, where chaos is planned.

Delicate Ecosystems in Glass

Beneath the glass dome, creatures plot and plan,
A snail writes a novel, with ink from a can.
A beetle wears glasses, reading the news,
While the moss tries to gossip about its woes.

The sun peeks inside, just to check on the fun,
Rays of laughter dart, like a playful little run.
The tiny trees giggle, waving their green,
In this fanciful realm, what a wacky scene!

There's a cactus in charge, with a prickly chair,
And a bristle fern waiting, with utmost flair.
While the flourished roots play hopscotch below,
The air is so thick, with this wild, leafy show.

With a sprinkle of water, the drama unfolds,
As seedlings tell tales that are silly and bold.
In this vivacious world, every whim takes flight,
Where laughter and growth bloom with pure delight.

The Dance of Light and Leaf

In corners of glass, where the shadows do creep,
A sunflower is snoring, tucked in with a peep.
The sunlight performs, a ballet on green,
As leaves stretch their arms, in a fabulous scene.

A spider's doing pirouettes, up on a stem,
While the roots are in rhythm, oh, look at them!
They shake and they shimmy, a festooned display,
In this miniature world, where nature holds sway.

The droplets of water, like diamonds below,
Encourage the leaves to put on a show.
The ferns give a bow, while sprouts take a spin,
In this living ballet, where giggles begin!

Clockwise or counter, the dance never stops,
A marveled audience of curious plots.
In a realm made of glass, with hope shining bright,
A celebration unfolds, under soft, glowing light.

A Treasure of Tiny Tales

Nestled in glass, a fairytale grows,
Each petal a whisper, each leaf gently glows.
There's a raccoon in pajamas, reading a book,
And a nerdy old turtle who loves how to cook.

Mice share their secrets, while birds take their flight,
In this whimsical setting, everything's bright.
The rabbits throw parties, with snacks from the sky,
As clouds drift on by, with a curious sigh.

The stories unfold, in snapshots so small,
Of friendship and laughter, that thrives through it all.
A snail tells a legend, about the great rain,
Which washed out the dirt but left treasures to gain.

With each little creature, a saga is spun,
In this world made of glass, where fantasy's fun.
It's a delightfully strange, fantastical place,
A treasure of tales, with a smile on each face.

Microcosms of Green Delight

In a jar, the plants play hide and seek,
Moss giggles when you hear it speak.
Snails wear hats, a tiny brigade,
In this green world, their laughter won't fade.

Sunlight dances on the glassy dome,
A buzz of life calls it 'home sweet home.'
Earthworms write poems, slightly absurd,
While crickets hold meetings without a word.

The pebbles gossip, the ferns engage,
A hamster once tried to join the stage.
With tiny spectacles, they read fine print,
In this living show, no need to squint.

So come, lend your ear to the verdant cries,
Where flora and fauna share silly highs.
In the glassy world, such stories unfold,
Each little critter, a joy to behold!

Twilight in Enclosed Realms

When the sun goes down, the fireflies glow,
A candlelit dance, just for show.
In the corners, shadows play peekaboo,
While the mushrooms toast to the evening dew.

Bugs don tuxedos, ready for a ball,
While lacy leaves sway, standing tall.
A beetle slips, oh what a sight,
He twirls and spins, with all his might.

The air is thick with whispers and cheer,
As the night unfolds, the fun draws near.
All gather 'round for a midnight snack,
Tiny donuts made from the trash out back!

So lift a glass—of soil, perhaps?
To the critters who tiptoe with moonlit chaps.
In this little realm, where silliness reigns,
Life's a comedy, free from all chains!

Secrets of the Living Glass

Behind glass walls, a kingdom thrives,
Tiny secrets where laughter derives.
The tendrils whisper of tales untold,
Adventures that sprout as the days unfold.

Spiders knitting their webs with flair,
Creating fashion with delicate care.
A leaf sneezes, and the world turns bright,
Chortles erupt, filling the night.

The earth giggles as raindrops fall,
"Not too much, or we'll drown them all!"
Bugs tell jokes that never grow old,
In this glass world, laughter is gold.

So peek into the glass, come join the fun,
As flora and fauna dance as one.
Life's little secrets, with giggles to share,
In this whimsical realm, there's joy everywhere!

The Art of Lush Isolation

In a glassy world, so snug and tight,
Frogs in tuxedos hop with delight.
A cactus debates with a leafy friend,
"Just because you're prickly doesn't mean the end!"

The soil holds stories, a rich, deep lore,
Of old plant parties and one failed war.
The ferns roll their eyes at the stubborn vines,
Who insist on climbing, despite tangled lines.

A ladybug sketches its plans in the dirt,
Puppetry dreams in a tiny pink shirt.
The geraniums gossip about the next show,
Where the lizard will dance—oh, what a glow!

With hidden laughter and pokey greens,
Life's quirks unfold, bursting at the seams.
In this isolated oasis, joy takes flight,
Where each little creature takes the stage at night!

Flora in Captivity

Tiny ferns in glassy beds,
Roots entwined like knitting threads.
Succulents sunbathe with flair,
Wondering who forgot the air.

A mossy kingdom under haze,
Sipping water through a maze.
Cacti chuckle at their pricks,
Holding hands with the salad mix.

Lily pads strike a pose,
While snails put on their rubber toes.
It's a party under dome,
With beetles dancing, feeling home.

Just a life in glassy glee,
Who needs freedom? Not a tree!
With every day, there's more to see,
In this eco-captive spree!

Lush Landscapes in Limbo

In a jar, life's bright and spry,
Plant friends waving, oh so spry.
Little soilworms have a say,
"Do we dig, or just delay?"

Leaves compete for the best light,
"I'm taller!" "No, I'm outta sight!"
Fungi laugh at their own space,
Mushroom hats bring such disgrace.

Waterfalls of droplets fall,
Miniature rivers, hear their call.
Fish made of plastic, swim with flair,
Just don't ask them to go anywhere.

It's a circus in this glass,
With makeshift paths for leaf and grass.
Lushness trapped within the dome,
A botanical jailhouse—oh, the tome!

Enigmatic Echoes of Earth

Seeds giggle in soft embrace,
Whispering secrets in this place.
Ferns and grasses play a game,
"Who's the tallest? Let's reclaim!"

Bubbles rise with a gentle plop,
Is that the sound of life, or stop?
Spider plants weave tales anew,
"Let's have fun in this debut!"

But what's that lurking in the shade?
A critter made of sweet charade?
Shrubs await a jungle jam,
As we all shout, "Here I am!"

Comedic chaos wrapped in glass,
Nature's circus, bringing sass.
Brightened fates, short on girth,
Echoes of life beneath the earth!

A Delicate Balance of Life

In crystal homes where critters crawl,
Each plant's a wallflower at the ball.
With roots that juggle, leaves that sway,
"Let's balance acts!" they shout and play.

The humidity's a sticky prank,
Moldy drama in that dank tank.
But what's a fern if not a star?
They throw their leaves and raise the bar!

Pests crash parties—what a sight,
"Get off my leaf!" they yell in fright.
Tiny roaches play the clown,
"Wet leaves? Who needs a crown?"

A delicate show, packed quite tight,
Where life finds laughter in its delight.
In this wild and quirky zone,
All thrive despite a tiny throne!

The Sacred Space of Soil and Stone

In a little jar of dirt and cheer,
Tiny creatures make their home so near.
A snail slides by, with a casual glide,
While a bit of moss tries to take him for a ride.

Stones chatter softly, secrets shared,
While earthworms giggle, never scared.
They throw a party, with roots and all,
And everyone's dancing, having a ball.

A bug dressed in blue puts on a show,
With grass as his stage, he steals the glow.
Laughing and lounging, a revelry grand,
In their sacred land, they dance hand in hand.

So raise a toast to this quirky tribe,
In steamy glass walls, they thrive and vibe.
A world so small, with mischief rife,
Who knew that dirt could hold such life?

Minimalist Gardens of Glass

Inside a cube, where air is confined,
Plants raise their hands, to feel so refined.
Cacti wear hats, quite oddly, you see,
While ferns laugh softly, "You're prickly, not me!"

A single leaf shouts, "Look, I'm a tree!"
The pebbles all roll, saying, "Let it be!"
In this glass palace, there's little to spare,
Yet joyfully green, they dance without care.

Spider plants wiggle, with flair and finesse,
Bidding farewell to the old garden mess.
While succulents smirk, over water tugs,
Sipping their drinks, like self-satisfied bugs.

With sunlight provided, they throw a grand bash,
Glass walls echo laughter, a colorful splash.
So here's to the garden, so sleek and small,
Where humor and nature completely enthrall.

Whims of the Enclosed Earth

In a jar so grand, where beetles debate,
A worm sings opera, oh isn't it great?
With a splash of soil, they hold a parade,
With daisies as marchers, none are afraid.

Tiny rocks giggle, as plants start to sway,
They created their world, in a comical way.
A frog at the corner, all princely and sly,
Pretends he's a king, with a very small tie.

Bubbles pop loudly, a drink for a bug,
Tiny ferns chuckle, sharing warm hugs.
In this cozy nook, they scheme and they play,
The day flies by like a whimsical ballet.

So here's to the wonders, in jars so benign,
Where nature and laughter perfectly align.
Just peep through the glass, and you soon will find,
A hilarious world, with humor entwined.

Wonders of the Whispering Glass

Behind the clear panes, secrets do twirl,
Where mushrooms wear caps, like boys with a whirl.
Caterpillars gossip, exchanging their dreams,
With laughter and joy as they plot their schemes.

In a corner, a snail, on a slow-motion race,
Wearing his shell like a fancy old vase.
While pebbles conspire, like wise little elves,
To throw a bash for their miniature selves.

A gecko makes faces, as he climbs on the wall,
Telling the plants, "I'm the best of them all!"
With a flick of his tongue, he snags a small fly,
Everyone chuckles, "Oh, now that's quite sly!"

So peer through the glass, and enjoy the display,
Of wonders contained, in a playful ballet.
A tiny utopia, with laughter and mirth,
In this magical land, full of life and worth.

A Symphony of Miniature Biomes

In a jar of dreams, plants sway with glee,
Tiny critters waltz, as if on spree.
Moss plays the harp, leaves dance in tune,
And a snail croons softly beneath the moon.

A frog on a lily, oh what a sight!
He practices opera, his voice takes flight.
Ants march like soldiers, in lines so neat,
While a spider conducts, tapping its feet.

Cacti wear hats, oh how they shine,
Succulents gossip, with gossip divine.
A worm in a tux, gives a bow and a spin,
With each little giggle, the party begins.

Not your usual concert, but laughter's the prize,
In this leafy jungle, joy always lies.
Who knew such fun could sprout and thrive,
In this tiny world, where all come alive?

Within the Crystal Enclosure

Behind the glass walls, a festivity's found,
In this miniature kingdom, laughter's unbound.
Goldfish in bow ties, flit around with ease,
While plants gossip softly, swaying in the breeze.

A tiny raccoon, wearing a hat made of leaves,
Steals snacks from a beetle; oh, what a tease!
The pebbles chuckle, the soil shakes with glee,
As they watch all the antics of their small jubilee.

Crickets in chorus start jamming away,
Each chirp like a note in a marvelous play.
Fireflies flicker, their lights gone a-wink,
As the cucumber beats provide all the sync.

In this sparkling world of frantic delight,
Where every small moment feels perfectly right,
Who knew that glass could hold such display?
Here's to the joy that never goes astray!

Nature's Smallest Sanctuary

In a tiny abode, where greens twist and twirl,
Residents bustle, giving life a whirl.
Mushrooms wear glasses, looking quite quaint,
While ladybugs argue, who's got more paint.

Squirrels with acorns, a feast for the show,
They debate a new recipe, butter or no?
The rocks sit around, sipping dew-colored tea,
While a hedgehog recites poetry with glee.

Lizards in tuxedos, striking a pose,
Compete in a dance-off, in front of the crows.
A butterfly DJ spins fun beats so fine,
And even the shy worm knows when to shine.

With giggles that echo through leaves on the ground,
This little ecosystem is quite the playground.
Who could have known, in such a small space,
Laughter and mischief would find their own place?

Dwellers of the Glass Abyss

In a deep little glass, funny antics arise,
Worms in full suits, adjusting their ties.
Frogs with top hats hop from one side to the next,
While spiders send texts, all feeling perplexed.

Ants with their briefcases march off to work,
Dodging a sneeze from a curious stork.
The pebbles are laughing, a cacophony sweet,
As the marbles roll over, dancing on feet.

Caterpillars gossip on leaves painted bright,
"Did you catch the last show? It was quite the sight!"
The fern takes a bow, while the soil claps loud,
In this comedic circus, we're all so proud.

Look in and behold, what chaos does dwell,
In this glassy abyss, all is funky and well.
A comedy club found in a plant-filled domain,
Where humor and nature both jointly reign.

Secrets of the Enclosed Ecosystem

Plants gossip away, quite the chatter,
Bugs dance around, like it's all that matters.
A snail creeps on, with a crown made of lettuce,
While a leaf whispers tales of the sun, oh what a fuss!

Pebbles argue who shines the most bright,
Moss rolls its eyes, says, 'I'm out of sight!'
In this little dome, secrets hide and play,
Who knew that roots could be so cliché?

The air is thick with laughter and light,
A lizard struts by, thinking it's quite the sight.
Tiny worlds flourished, yet not a care,
In this whimsical glass, life's seldom unfair.

So gather around, peek through the glass,
Join the tale of turf, where no grasses pass.
In a world so small, such joy we find,
Nature's giggles echo, entwined and unlined.

Microcosmic Whimsy

Inside this glass, a party's in swing,
With earthworms as DJs, just listen to them sing!
Fungi wear hats made of moist, furry bread,
While butterflies tweet, spreading giggles instead.

A beetle's got moves, like it's busting a groove,
While succulents sway, making the room move.
Dancing in circles, they twirl and they glide,
Under the canopy, where critters collide.

Crickets tell jokes, with rhymes full of zest,
While cacti share gossip on who looks the best.
Tiny trees giggle, with branches that sway,
In this wild, leafy rave, joy's here to stay!

So take a deep look, in this playful air,
Where each little inhabitant has talent to share.
In a landscape so small, laughter abounds,
Microcosmic foolishness knows no bounds.

Roots and Shoots in Seclusion

Roots take refuge, with secrets to share,
Under the soil, like they haven't a care.
A shoot pokes out, saying, 'Look at me sprout!'
While worms roll their eyes, thinking it's all a rout.

A spider spins tales of high-flying stars,
While leaves join in chorus, like tiny guitars.
Grass in the shadows, with wisdom so deep,
Whispers of dreams that won't let them sleep.

In this tiny realm, mischief's a breeze,
With ladybugs plotting beneath the tall trees.
A wild little party, with no end in sight,
As roots tap their toes to the rhythm of light.

They giggle at sunlight, they shuffle in shade,
This secluded gathering, a symphony made.
With whispers of fun, they all play their roles,
While this secret oasis hums deep in their souls.

The Art of Subtropical Serenity

In a cozy corner, where chaos meets calm,
Ferns hold a seminar on growing a palm.
A snail's on a mission, with a map that's all wrong,
While a frog croaks a tune, and the flies hum along.

Succulent dreams of a cactus parade,
Under arching branches, bright colors displayed.
A tiny lizard's setting fashion trends,
In this leafy lounge, where laughter transcends.

The air is a canvas, painted soft green,
With jokes and good vibes, it's quite the scene.
Plants trade their stories, with roots intertwined,
Creating a haven, no judgment in kind.

So relish the whispers of life's merry spree,
In subtropical charm, come laugh with me.
A world full of quirks, let joy be the theme,
In this artful enclave, we live and we dream.

Echoes of Glass Gardens

In a box of glass, the plants do dance,
Tiny bugs hold an awkward romance.
A squirrel peeps in with a curious eye,
Wondering why the ferns just won't fly.

The cactus grins, it's quite the prick,
While the ferns are trapped, feeling quite sick.
A snail tells tales of the world outside,
While a timid worm tries to find its pride.

The moss has dreams of a grand escape,
While the soil giggles, feeling quiteape.
Each leaf whispers jokes, like it's a stand-up,
As the sun beams down with a warming cup.

Glass echoes laughter, a comical scene,
In this little world, where the odd are seen.
The plants and bugs form a silly crew,
With adventures that offer quite the view.

Secrets Beneath the Dome

Underneath the dome, a secret lies,
A plant with gossip and twinkling eyes.
The potbelly mushroom serves tea to a lizard,
While rumors spread like a wild blizzard.

The fern tells tales of its wild cousin,
Who dreams of freedom but feels quite bustin'.
The spider weaves webs of intricate tales,
Of far-off gardens and endless trails.

A rogue radish claims it can dance on its head,
While the timid thyme wishes it were dead.
Each little critter, with stories to share,
Makes this dome of secrets a comical affair.

So beneath the glass, life's a circus show,
With plants and bugs putting on the best glow.
Secrets unfold in this quirky space,
Where laughter blooms with a curious grace.

Whispers in a Greenhouse

In the quiet corners, whispers collide,
As plants share secrets, with humorous pride.
A radish jokes about its unexpected weight,
While the herbs compete for the best on a plate.

The mints giggle and spread their delight,
As a curious beetle takes off in flight.
A flower, flamboyant, acts quite the diva,
While the leaves chuckle, wishing they could leave ya.

With every breeze, tales waft through the air,
A spider's acrobatics draw laughter to share.
The garden gnome listens, a wise little sage,
As the vegetables plot from their leafy stage.

In this whimsical world beneath glass and vine,
Nature's own comedy, perfectly fine.
A symphony of chuckles with each funny sight,
In the whispers of a greenhouse, comedic and bright.

Sheltered Breaths of Nature

Under glass, the world feels cozy yet weird,
As the plants stir awake, quite curious and cheered.
A sunflower leans in, with a wink and a grin,
While the shy little sprout hopes to grow with kin.

Tales of the outside are shared over tea,
As the cucumbers dream of being fancy and free.
A snail slides by, slow as a tale,
While the daisies gossip, pretending to wail.

The soil chuckles, boasting tales of old,
Of seeds once scattered, now growing bold.
Each leaf's a comedian, cracking sweet jokes,
In this cozy corner, joy quietly provokes.

So gather 'round, in this glassy embrace,
Where every green being finds its own space.
Breaths of nature, wrapped in delight,
Sheltered in humor, under day and night.

www.ingramcontent.com/pod-product-compliance
Lightning Source LLC
Chambersburg PA
CBHW072130070526
44585CB00016B/1602